CALLING
GOD
NAMES

CALLING GOD NAMES

Seven Names of God That Reveal His Character

NORMAN HUBBARD

NAVPRESS
Discipleship Inside Out®

NAVPRESS
Discipleship Inside Out®

NavPress is the publishing ministry of The Navigators, an international Christian organization and leader in personal spiritual development. NavPress is committed to helping people grow spiritually and enjoy lives of meaning and hope through personal and group resources that are biblically rooted, culturally relevant, and highly practical.

**For a free catalog go to www.NavPress.com
or call 1.800.366.7788 in the United States or 1.800.839.4769 in Canada.**

© 2013 by Norman Hubbard

All rights reserved. No part of this publication may be reproduced in any form without written permission from NavPress, P.O. Box 35001, Colorado Springs, CO 80935. www.navpress.com

NAVPRESS and the NAVPRESS logo are registered trademarks of NavPress. Absence of ® in connection with marks of NavPress or other parties does not indicate an absence of registration of those marks.

NavPress titles may be purchased in bulk for ministry, educational, business, fund-raising, or sales promotional use. For information, please call NavPress Special Markets at 1.800.504.2924.

ISBN-13: 978-1-61747-835-2

Cover design by Arvid Wallen
Cover image by Eugene Ivanov

Some of the anecdotal illustrations in this book are true to life and are included with the permission of the persons involved. All other illustrations are composites of real situations, and any resemblance to people living or dead is coincidental.

Unless otherwise identified, all Scripture quotations in this publication are taken from The Holy Bible, English Standard Version (ESV), copyright © 2001 by Crossway Bibles, a division of Good News Publishers. Used by permission. All rights reserved. Other versions used include: the New American Standard Bible® (NASB), Copyright © 1960, 1962, 1963, 1968, 1971, 1972, 1973, 1975, 1977, 1995 by The Lockman Foundation. Used by permission; the *Holy Bible, New International Version*® (NIV®), Copyright © 1973, 1978, 1984 by Biblica, used by permission of Zondervan, all rights reserved; the New King James Version (NKJV). Copyright © 1982 by Thomas Nelson, Inc. Used by permission. All rights reserved; and *The New Testament in Modern English* (PH), J. B. Phillips Translator, © J. B. Phillips 1958, 1960, 1972, used by permission of Macmillan Publishing Company.

Printed in the United States of America

1 2 3 4 5 6 7 8 / 17 16 15 14 13

To my parents, Larry and Claire Hubbard,
who raised me to honor the name of the Lord,
prayed for me when I didn't,
and trusted in the Most High when times were hard.

Great and amazing are your deeds,

O Lord God the Almighty!

Just and true are your ways,

O King of the nations!

Who will not fear, O Lord,

and glorify your name?

For you alone are holy.

All nations will come

and worship you,

for your righteous acts have been revealed.

—Revelation 15:3-4

CONTENTS

WHAT'S IN A NAME?

I took a calculated risk at the beach when I was fifteen years old. I changed my name. A suave, tan, cool teenager, I was prowling the Myrtle Beach strip in search of would-be girlfriends. The name Norman just didn't fit. It called up images of a skinny, nerdy kid, and I was only skinny . . . and tan.

So I changed my name to Wes.

This identity change was a stroke of genius and required very little justification. My middle name actually is Wesley, so I wasn't lying or telling people to call me by a pseudonym. I really was Wesley, but I had never been called anything except Norman. In fact, I wasn't even sure I knew how to spell Wesley. Even so, I reasoned that no one on the beach would ask me how to spell my name, especially not if I introduced myself as Wes.

So it was that I became Wes for two days. I met a group of teenagers at a dance club one night, told them all that my name was Wes, and got along swimmingly with them until the next day. As I was walking along the beach, taking in the sun, salt, and activity, someone ran up and tapped me on the shoulder. When I turned to see who it was, a girl I had met the night before was staring at me.

"Are you deaf or daydreaming?" she asked playfully. "We've all been shouting at you."

I turned to see a number of the friends I had met the night before, and it struck me that several people had been yelling, "Wes! Wes!" as I walked by.

"I guess I wasn't paying attention," I answered unconvincingly. The red in my face had nothing to do with the summer sun.

As quickly as I could extricate myself from that group of friends, I decided to revert to my original name. Nerdy though it might sound, it was better than looking like I was an absent-minded or unfriendly guy named Wes.

Have you ever been hailed by a name not your own? How did you respond? Did you say to yourself, *I'm sure that person means well. Why not simply go by Abner (or Angelica) for a time?*

Chances are, you politely correct people when they call you by the wrong name, for the fact of the matter is that you have a particular name. You are who you are, and your name is not an arbitrary accessory, like a hat, that can be swapped out at intervals.

The same thing is true of the God who created this world and sent His Son to redeem it. He has revealed Himself by name to His people and has chosen to exalt His name and His Word above all things (see Psalm 138:2).

Bearing this in mind, we should call out to God in prayer according to the names He has revealed to us. We should no more expect God to turn around and answer us when we address Him improperly than we should expect a guy named Thomas to turn around when someone yells out, "Hey, Sue!" But if He does (because He is merciful), we should expect Him to correct our mistake.

What is more, God has given us a rich vocabulary with which to praise Him. "Shout for joy to God, all the earth; *sing the glory of his name*; give to him glorious praise!" (Psalm 66:1-2, emphasis added). What a grace to be able to call God by name as we worship. What a challenge to testify about Him among our friends and neighbors, indeed "all the earth," as we call God names!

USING THIS STUDY

The seven sessions that make up this book will help shape your private prayer, public worship, and personal witness as you study the Scriptures.

In short, you will know God better because you will know Him by name. Of course, you'll have to open your mind, your Bible, and your schedule if you want to learn well the lessons that follow.

Each chapter of this study follows a structure similar to this:

- An introduction to orient you to the name of God you'll be studying
- A study of two or more Scripture passages that show how God revealed Himself by name to Israel, how Jesus helped us develop our understanding of God's nature, and/or how we should relate to God on the basis of His name
- A section called "Trust This Truth," which helps you consider how knowing God's name affects your life of prayer, worship, and witness
- A section called "Memorize This Message," which offers a verse for you to take to heart, think about, and commit to memory
- A section called "Worship in These Words," which offers a hymn or poem that exalts God for the truths you've studied

This study is designed first of all for you as an individual. Take the time you need. Because you'll study several passages in each chapter, you will probably want to spread your study over several days. Keep asking, *So what? What difference does this make to me today?*

If you're studying with a group, set a pace that works well for everyone. This could mean taking one chapter per week or two weeks per chapter. Group members will need to do the Bible study portion of the chapter (which means everything before "Trust This Truth") on their own before the group meets. That individual work will probably take at least ninety minutes. Then when the group gathers, you don't need to share answers to every Bible study question. Instead, invite people to share the main things they learned from each passage they studied.

Discuss the questions in "Trust This Truth" together. Because these questions deal with each of you personally, they will be fruitful for group discussion.

Thus, a lively discussion of chapter 1 ("The Holy One") might go like this:

- What is one of the main things you learned about the nearness of the Holy One in Exodus 19?
- How would you explain to someone what God meant when He said, "Be holy, for I am holy"?
- We would expect God to separate Himself from sinners utterly. But how did the prophet Hosea characterize the Holy One's commitment to Israel?
- What role does the Holy Spirit play in helping us live a life of holiness?
- What do you think it means to walk by the Spirit?
- What are two practices you have found most helpful in your endeavors to walk by the Spirit? What are two barriers to your doing so?
- How do you think your prayers, worship, or witness will change as a result of what you've learned about the Holy One?

If a lively and life-transforming discussion of the Scriptures is your aim, let thorough, personal preparation before each meeting be your rule. Everyone benefits from the insight each person brings.

1

THE HOLY ONE

Who Is Like No Other in Radiant Purity

For thus says the One who is high and lifted up, who inhabits eternity, whose name is Holy: "I dwell in the high and holy place, and also with him who is of a contrite and lowly spirit, to revive the spirit of the lowly, and to revive the heart of the contrite."

ISAIAH 57:15

GAZING THROUGH A PINHOLE

Very early in life, I showed my true colors as a child destined for the liberal arts. When my science teacher informed my class that a lunar eclipse was imminent, I was startlingly disinterested in how it was going to happen. Instead, I was almost undone by the fact that the moon's light was going to simply disappear on a given night. In the realm of childhood fascination, there is seldom room for tedious explanation.

Imagine then my transport when, later in school, I learned that a solar eclipse was coming and that *you can't look at an eclipse of the sun without going blind.* It was hard to comprehend. There seemed to be greater danger in looking at the sun when its light was obscured than when it was shining in full strength. I later learned the tedious explanation for this, but my immediate impression upon hearing that you can go blind from looking at a darkened sun was one of unmitigated wonder.

The world of science had nothing to offer me in light of so great a mystery—nothing, that is, until my teacher went on to explain how we could go home and make a "pinhole camera" to observe an image of the eclipse. Immediately, I jumped ship on the liberal arts and devoted myself entirely to industry and engineering. I would make a pinhole camera to gaze at the dangerously dark sun.

Like other construction projects I've attempted, my pinhole camera fell somewhat short of my expectations. In fact, I can't even remember whether it worked. The solar eclipse of 1984 was only partial in South Carolina, and I was probably expecting an eclipse much longer, darker, and more magical than the data warranted.

My project flopped, and my imagination was fired. I later became an English major.

I still haven't gotten over the fact that we live in a galactic neighborhood with a star so brilliant that you can't even look at it when it's darkened. To gaze at our sun, we need some intermediary, like a solar lens or a pinhole camera, which will make the brightness bearable or transpose the great orb into some smaller reflection.

As it is with the sun, so it is with our God. He is veiled from our sight not because He is distant but because He is brilliant. He actually obscures Himself (see Isaiah 45:15) lest we gaze on Him directly and find ourselves undone (see Exodus 33:20). We should be grateful for the eclipse of God and perhaps more grateful for the "pinhole camera" of the Bible. By gazing into it, we can see Him reflected in terms we can understand.

No term better captures the essence of God's transcendent purity, His unspeakable otherness, than the word *holiness*. Not merely a description of God, *holiness* is actually His name—"For thus says the high and exalted One . . . whose name is Holy" (Isaiah 57:15, NASB). God is the Holy One, and if we hope to have a relationship with Him, we will have to share in His holiness. But how can that be? How can we who are fallen share His moral purity, which will pull us from the pollution of a fallen world?

Even though God dwells in a "high and holy place," He also dwells with those "of a contrite and lowly spirit" (Isaiah 57:15). In the Old Testament, we read of the call to be holy as God is holy. In the New Testament, we read about how this is possible. The Holy One sent His Son to represent us in His life and death. Through faith in Him, we share in God's holiness as God shares with us His Holy Spirit.

HAVING THE HOLY ONE NEAR

When God delivered Israel from Egypt, there was no question in anyone's mind that the God of Israel had moved in the midst of His people. However, no one in the exodus generation thought of God as someone to get chummy with. Moses might have spoken with God "face to face, as a man speaks to his friend" (Exodus 33:11), but God showed up at these meetings in a pillar of cloud and fire, while all Israel stood and worshipped Him (see Exodus 33:10).

On the day God called Moses up Mount Sinai to receive the Law, Israel got a lesson in God's holiness. Though He is not referred to explicitly as the Holy One in this biblical passage, His radiant purity and transcendent otherness cannot be missed. Read Exodus 19:1-23.

1. As Israel made its way out of bondage in Egypt and toward the land of promise, the LORD said, "I bore you on eagles' wings and brought you *to myself*" (verse 4, emphasis added). Describe the way God intended to elevate His people in this relationship, according to verses 5-6.

2. How did the people of Israel respond to God's gracious invitation?

3. In verse 9, God wanted the people to hear Him speak with Moses so that they would believe him. Why, then, do you suppose that He veiled Himself in a cloud and demanded that the people stay off the mountain where He was meeting with Moses?

4. The end of verse 9 says, "Moses told the words of the people to the LORD." According to verse 8, what response had they made to God's covenant promises?

_____

▶ Sometime after Moses ascended Mount Sinai to receive the Law, he recorded the words of the Law on scrolls. These scrolls were augmented by the inspired writings of other prophets in Israel. The Jewish Scriptures of the Old Testament and the authoritative writings of the New Testament began, in time, circulating as a single book. Chances are, the cover or title page of your Bible declares itself to be *The* Holy *Bible.* Have you ever thought about what that description means?

_____

5. According to verses 10-12 and 14-15, describe the preparation process the people had to go through for three days before Moses ascended Mount Sinai to meet with the Lord.

6. The penalty for overstepping the boundary set up around Mount Sinai was death (see verses 12-13). What message do you think this severe punishment was meant to communicate?

7. It seems reasonable that the trembling people of Israel would back as far away from Mount Sinai as possible, especially on "the morning of the third day [when] there were thunders and lightnings and a thick cloud on the mountain and a very loud trumpet blast" (verse 16). Yet they were not supposed to back away. Where was Israel to stand on the third day, and why do you suppose this was so (see verse 17)?

8. Place yourself among the people of Israel at the foot of Mount Sinai that day. Would you feel confident or concerned? Explain why.

9. While reading about a scene as dramatic as this one, we must not lose sight of God's overall purposes. (He wasn't simply showing off His pyrotechnic abilities.) What was He trying to communicate about Himself with the fire, smoke, and thunder on Sinai?

10. In Exodus 19, God was preparing His people to receive His Law. Throughout that Law, God repeated a similar refrain to Israel. You'll find a representative passage in Leviticus 11:44-45. Read it and then fill in the blanks below:

    "Be _____, for I am _____."

11. Based on their experiences with God at Mount Sinai, what would you say are some things Israel would have known about God's holy presence at this point in history?

12. Given what you know about holiness from this passage or prior instruction, how would you explain the command to "be holy" to someone unfamiliar with the term?

▶ It is one thing to observe the radiant purity of God on display at Sinai. But how are we to be holy as God is holy? "To be holy," writes author Jerry Bridges, "is to be morally blameless. It is to be separated from sin and, therefore, consecrated to God."[1]

THE HOLY ONE DOES NOT REJECT US

Very soon after their experience at Sinai, the people proved that their actual commitment to holiness fell far short of their stated intentions. They regularly rejected God's rules and went their own way. It would make sense that a holy God would then purge them from His presence or withdraw from them, right? With only Exodus 19 to guide us, we might draw that conclusion, but we've got the rest of the Scripture to show us a fuller picture.

God is not quick to judge unholy people. He prefers to call out to them, warn them, and even discipline them rather than cut them off completely. And His holiness certainly does not prohibit Him from dwelling in the midst of His people. The Holy One doesn't have to sit in a corner because we are all bad. Rather, He is personally present in His universe, dealing with the unholiness He cannot bear in the people He will not forsake.

The book of Hosea helps us see how a holy God relates to an unholy people, in this case Ephraim, an alternative name God used for the people of Israel. (Ephraim was the largest tribe in the northern kingdom of Israel.) This prophecy is set just before the time when the northern kingdom of Israel was attacked and sent into exile by the kingdom of Assyria. Read Hosea 11:1-11.

13. According to Hosea 11:1-4, how did God demonstrate His love for Israel in its early days—"when Israel was a child"?

14. In what ways did Israel respond to the kind ministries of God?

15. God foretold a time when Israel would again be oppressed by a hostile world power, Assyria, as they were by Egypt in times past (see verses 5 and 11). Yet the light of hope for Israel did not go out altogether, for God also told how He would be deeply moved for

His people in times to come. How would you describe God's commitment to Israel, as expressed in verses 8-9?

16. In verse 9, God declared, "I will not execute my burning anger; I will not again destroy Ephraim; for I am God and not a man." What contrast was God drawing between His ways with Israel and the ways in which a person might react in similar circumstances?

17. Having spurned God's love and experienced His purifying judgments, consisting of defeat and exile at the hands of the Assyrians, where was Israel to look for the Holy One to dwell in the day of their restoration (see verse 9)?

18. What impressions of the Holy One do you take away from Hosea 11:1-11?

TRUST THIS TRUTH

The Law that Moses received from the Lord on Mount Sinai (Exodus 19) beckons us to be holy, but it doesn't bestow on us the power to be holy. It can show us what holiness looks like, which is important, but we need more.

As Christians, we have more. "But by [God's] doing you are in Christ Jesus, who became to us wisdom from God, and righteousness and sanctification, and redemption" (1 Corinthians 1:30, NASB). Holiness (or "sanctification") is our present possession in Christ Jesus. To say it another way, "By [God's] will, we have been made holy through the sacrifice of the body of Jesus Christ once for all" (Hebrews 10:10, NIV).

Because of Christ's sacrifice, holiness is our present possession. Because the Holy Spirit lives within us, holiness is to be our present experience. We possess holiness in Christ, and we express it daily through the influence of the Holy Spirit.

For Christians, holiness is not an abstraction but a person. Our share in divine holiness doesn't involve us in weak attempts at moral behavior through human strength. God has shared His holiness with us by sharing Himself with us in the person of His Son and the indwelling presence of His Spirit.

▶ The Old Testament was written over a period of two thousand years, during which time the Spirit of God was referred to as "the Holy Spirit" in only *two* passages: Psalm 51:11 and Isaiah 63:10. Contrast that with the New Testament, which was written over a period of about sixty years. During this time, the Spirit of God was referred to as "the Holy Spirit" in *eighty-nine* passages!

The Old Testament prophets had foretold, "I will put my Spirit within you, and cause you to walk in my statutes and be careful to obey my rules" (Ezekiel 36:27). They saw that God would fill His people with His Spirit.

And so it happened to the church at Pentecost. As all the believers gathered in Jerusalem, young and old, men and women were filled with the Holy Spirit and enabled to testify about God's marvelous works in languages they had never studied. Peter interpreted the phenomenon thus: "This is what was uttered through the prophet Joel: 'And in the last days it shall be . . . that I will pour out my Spirit on all flesh'" (Acts 2:16-17).

The Old Testament prophets set the expectations, and the New Testament Scriptures announced the fulfillment of God's promise. All who are in Christ share in God's holy nature because He dwells in us by His Spirit. For the purposes of this study, you might think of the Holy Spirit as the Holy One dwelling within us.

19. What kind of ministry can we expect "the Holy One dwelling within us" to have in our lives? The following verses help to answer this question.

Passage	What kind of ministry does "the Holy One dwelling within us" have in our lives?
The Helper, the Holy Spirit, whom the Father will send in my name, he will teach you all things and bring to your remembrance all that I have said to you. (John 14:26)	
You will receive power when the Holy Spirit has come upon you, and you will be my witnesses in Jerusalem and in all Judea and Samaria, and to the end of the earth. (Acts 1:8)	

Passage	What kind of ministry does "the Holy One dwelling within us" have in our lives?
God has done what the law, weakened by the flesh, could not do. By sending his own Son in the likeness of sinful flesh and for sin, he condemned sin in the flesh, in order that the righteous requirement of the law might be fulfilled in us, who walk not according to the flesh but according to the Spirit. (Romans 8:3-4)	
We all, with unveiled face, beholding the glory of the Lord, are being transformed into the same image from one degree of glory to another. For this comes from the Lord who is the Spirit. (2 Corinthians 3:18)	
We ought always to give thanks to God for you, brothers beloved by the Lord, because God chose you as the firstfruits to be saved, through sanctification by the Spirit and belief in the truth. (2 Thessalonians 2:13)	

20. God shares His holiness with us by sharing Himself with us in the Holy Spirit. But this indwelling involves relationship, and as with any relationship, something will be required of us beyond a passive acceptance of a mysterious union. In Galatians 5:25, Paul put it this way: "If we live by the Spirit, let us also walk by the Spirit" (NASB). What do you think it means to "walk by" (or keep in step with) the Spirit?

21. What are two practices you have found helpful in your endeavors to walk by the Spirit?

22. What are two things that have been barriers to your doing so?

MEMORIZE THIS MESSAGE

For thus says the One who is high and lifted up, who inhabits eternity, whose name is Holy: "I dwell in the high and holy place, and also with him who is of a contrite and lowly spirit, to revive the spirit of the lowly, and to revive the heart of the contrite." (Isaiah 57:15)

WORSHIP IN THESE WORDS

When we focus on God's holiness, our thoughts and behavior are drawn toward Him by grace, but when we lose sight of it, our thoughts and behavior are dragged downward. Songs like "Holy, Holy, Holy!" help us keep a sharp eye and a reverent heart fixed on the Holy One.

You may sing or recite this hymn in your private devotions or during your small-group meeting. If no one is familiar with the tune or cares to strike it up for the group, the stanzas can be read aloud as one would read a poem.

▶ The hymn "Holy, Holy, Holy!" is taken from Isaiah 6:1-3, in which the prophet saw a vision of God's throne room. As part of this vision, angels veiled their eyes and feet as they sang out, "Holy, holy, holy is the LORD of hosts; the whole earth is full of his glory!" (verse 3). These angels are specifically called seraphs, a term derived from a Hebrew word meaning "to burn." The most brilliant angels of heaven could not outshine the Holy One, but rather they shielded their eyes from His resplendent holiness.

"Holy, Holy, Holy!"
Words by Reginald Heber

Holy, holy, holy! Lord God Almighty!
Early in the morning our song shall rise to Thee.
Holy, holy, holy! Merciful and mighty,
God in three persons, blessed Trinity!

Holy, holy, holy! All the saints adore Thee,
Casting down their golden crowns around the glassy sea;
Cherubim and seraphim falling down before Thee,
Which wert, and art, and evermore shall be.

Holy, holy, holy! Though the darkness hide Thee,
Though the eye of sinful man Thy glory may not see,
Only Thou art holy; there is none beside Thee,
Perfect in power, in love and purity.

Holy, holy, holy! Lord God Almighty!
All Thy works shall praise Thy Name, in earth, and sky, and sea.
Holy, holy, holy! Merciful and mighty,
God in three persons, blessed Trinity![2]

2

THE MOST HIGH

Who Reigns Over All the Forces Influencing Your Life

I will be glad and exult in you; I will sing praise to your name, O Most High.

PSALM 9:2

KING OF THE HILL

A multimillion-dollar marketing industry has sprung up around parents to divert their attention from this one simple fact: Most children are happiest when playing in a big pile of dirt. Not only is dirt dirty and thus filled with promise, but a big pile of dirt offers limitless possibilities for play.

Dump eight yards of topsoil in your backyard, and here's what you'll find. Without changing into play clothes or out of their new shoes, children will run out of the house and scramble up the hill. Because a pile of fresh dirt is soft, they'll invariably begin jumping or rolling around in it. Fresh dirt also invites children to dig. The prospect of moving so much earth around with small shovels or sticks is delightful to children who are generally limited to moving around on top of the hard ground.

If you leave children in the dirt long enough, though, a spontaneous game of King of the Hill is bound to happen. If you're unfamiliar with the game, the rules are quite simple. One person attains a position on top of the hill, and everyone else tries to push him off. To defend himself, the King of the Hill responds in kind by pushing other people down.

While safety is not a primary concern in King of the Hill, children do learn valuable lessons about life (especially corporate life) in the game. The following list is illustrative, not exhaustive:

1. Usually the biggest, most aggressive person is King of the Hill.
2. The person at the top of the hill enjoys a distinct advantage over everyone under him.
3. Though a dirt mound is soft, it's still unpleasant to be flung down it by a big, aggressive person.
4. Two or more small people can form a temporary alliance to topple the King of the Hill.
5. Temporary alliances rarely hold when two or more people attain the top of the hill.

Lessons like these can help kids understand something of the fallen realm of relationships they'll inherit someday, but the experiences can mislead as well. Who is, after all, the King of the Hill? Ask any adult, and they'll definitely say, "Not me." Most of us feel like we've tried the ascent several times and found ourselves bounced back down on our bottoms by unfriendly people and unfortunate circumstances.

We might not be able to say with certainty, but we feel there are forces at the top slinging us around with no scruples about doing what's in our best interest. This, of course, is not the Christian answer—it has nothing to do with the Scriptures—but it's the one that feels true to experience. Ask anyone nursing bruises from bad choices, bad luck, or bad people—at the bottom of the hill.

The only problem with this supposition is that experiences do not teach us anything *of themselves*. Instead, people interpret the significance of their experiences and draw their own conclusions. "Who's at the top of the hill?" Experience doesn't answer that question. We do.

To do so accurately, we've got to turn our attention from the dirt mound to the Bible, looking beyond our limited experiences of falling down in a fallen world to a body of knowledge more reliable than our own. When we do, we encounter the assertion that "the Most High God rules the kingdom of mankind" (Daniel 5:21).

Of course, this is what we'd expect the Bible to say. But we might not appreciate just how personally God takes the point. He doesn't just exercise sovereignty—He calls Himself "the Most High," and He expects His people to call Him by this name and relate to Him and His world accordingly.

God is at the top of the hill. We might have bruises at the bottom of it, but our bruises are not our best instructors. Let us look to the Scriptures, to the revelation of the Most High, and let Him guide us to the truth. "Send out your light and your truth; let them lead me; let them bring me to your holy hill and to your dwelling!" (Psalm 43:3).

THE KNOWLEDGE OF THE MOST HIGH

The first person to refer to God as "the Most High" in Scripture was an ancient priest who was, curiously, not a Jew or even a forebear of the Jews. Instead, he was a mysterious man named Melchizedek who came out to bless Abram, the soon-to-be father of the Jewish people, after a battle. Read Genesis 14:18-24.

1. By what titles was Melchizedek identified in Genesis 14:18?

2. For what attributes did Melchizedek praise God in Genesis 14:19-20?

> Sodom was the town God later destroyed with fire and burning sulfur from the sky because of its exceeding evil. Melchizedek's home city of Salem enjoyed a far happier fate. Salem eventually became Jerusalem, the capital city of the Jews and site of the temple built in King Solomon's time.

3. At the end of Genesis 14:20, Abram gave Melchizedek a tenth (or "tithe") of the spoils of war. Abram, would not, however, receive any payment from the king of Sodom (see verses 21-24) even though Abram had recovered the king's people and property. Why was Abram willing to give a tithe to the priest of God Most High but unwilling to receive payment for his military support?

> Melchizedek's name crops up only once more in the Old Testament—in a prophetic psalm in which the Lord swore to His Messiah, "You are a priest forever after the order of Melchizedek" (Psalm 110:4). That prophecy remained uninterpreted throughout history until the writer of Hebrews revealed how the king-priest Melchizedek foreshadowed Jesus. You can read all about it in Hebrews 7.

4. If this was the only instance of the name "God Most High" in the Bible, what conclusions could you draw about His nature?

DEVOTION OR DISTANCE?

In his notes on Genesis 14, the commentator Albert Barnes remarked that "the unity, the omnipotence, and the absolute pre-eminence of God were still living in the memory and conscience of a section . . . of the inhabitants of this land."[1] In other words, it wasn't just a single clan who worshipped the Most High in the region of Canaan, but this knowledge of God was diffused throughout a part of the world. We see this demonstrated again when Balaam, another Gentile prophet-priest, claimed to know "the knowledge of the Most High" (Numbers 24:16). Thus, the story of the Bible begins with two Gentiles acknowledging the Most High. Fortunately, though, the revelation doesn't end there.

▶ Ancient inscriptions in the Middle East suggest that other nations might have worshipped a deity called Elyon, the supreme god among lesser deities. However, the Scriptures show that the Jews had a different idea. "[In] reference to God, *elyon* is never preceded by the article *ha-* ("the"), [therefore] it must have been regarded as a proper noun, a name of God."[2]

God is sovereign over all the earth. Many ancient peoples knew it, but the Jews preserved and amplified this understanding through their divinely inspired writings. A concept so lofty could lose touch with the earth pretty quickly, though. That is why a group of poets wrote a song to instruct Jews and Gentiles alike about how to respond to the reality of God's rule. Read Psalm 47.

5. Who is being beckoned to worship the Lord in the opening two verses of this psalm?

6. How and why should they do so, according to the psalmist?

7. Describe God's relation to Israel as given in verses 3-4? What reasons do His people have for praising Him?

8. The imagery in verse 5 suggests a victorious king returning to Jerusalem after battle. The Most High has come down to deal with Israel's enemies in battle and "has gone up with a shout" (verse 5). How should the King's people respond to His sovereign power over the nations?

9. If the imagery of the early verses in the psalm have to do with battle, the final two verses present quite a different vision of the future, one in which harmony prevails. Who will be assembled before the throne of God? What will their relation to God be?

▶ Regarding the universality of God's rule and the extent of His redemptive influence, Paul said, "Is God the God of Jews only? Is He not the God of Gentiles also? Yes, of Gentiles also, since God is one — who will justify the circumcised by faith and the uncircumcised through faith" (Romans 3:29-30).

10. Psalm 47 helps us know how all people ought to respond to the victorious reign of God. However, our reactions aren't always so righteous. Place a mark by any of the sentences below that describe how you've felt about God's sovereignty.

- God has seemed so highly exalted that I can't see how He is involved in my life on a daily basis. He's more like a distant ideal than a presently ruling King.
- I am certain of God's reign but equally certain I've not lived according to His rules. Thus, I'd rather keep my distance from the Most High, who is "to be feared" (Psalm 47:2).
- The difficulties I have faced make me wonder whether God does indeed reign supreme or whether "time and chance" (Ecclesiastes 9:11) sometimes get their way in spite of His best intentions.

11. Describe one of your life experiences that has inclined you to the view above.

12. According to the psalmist, God's highness shouldn't make us feel distance or despair but devotion. The psalmist's word choice is graphic and instructive. We should "clap [our] hands" (47:1), "shout to God with loud songs of joy" (verse 1), and "sing praises with understanding" (verse 7, NKJV). How might this kind of wholehearted, intelligent worship steer us into a full embrace of God's sovereign rule?

13. If you leave this study thinking, "Singing praises to the Most High is a very noble idea, and I ought to try it sometime," you probably never will. What are some practical measures you might take to put more time and heart into worshipping the Most High?

ABIDING IN THE SHELTER OF THE MOST HIGH

The one who knows God as the Most High will not only praise Him but run to Him for refuge in times of trouble—and stay there. Read Psalm 91 (and take note of the names for God used in the first two verses).

The psalmist opened the psalm this way:

He who dwells in the shelter of the Most High
will abide in the shadow of the Almighty.

I will say to the LORD, "My refuge and my fortress,
my God, in whom I trust." (verses 1-2)

14. Give some thought to a current situation in which you feel
    exposed, like your well-being is on the line. In the space below,
    write out a prayer to the Most High, beginning with the words of
    Psalm 91:1-2. Be sure to mention your difficult circumstances in
    your prayer, but end your prayer by affirming God's greatness and
    goodness even when you find His ways hard to discern.

15. Psalm 91 begins with a man expressing his commitment to the
    Most High, just as you have done in the prayer above. But
    the psalm ends with the Most High expressing His commitment
    to the person praying. To whom did God make His promises
    in Psalm 91:14?

16. In the context of the psalm and in light of your present circum-
    stances, what might it mean to know God's name?

17. Earlier in the psalm, we read that "no evil shall be allowed to befall" the one who has made the Most High his refuge (verses 9-10). However, in verse 15 the Lord promised to be with the same person in times of trouble. How would you explain this contrast?

▶ The ministry and majesty of Jesus come to mind in this psalm, not only because Satan misused verse 11 to tempt Jesus in the wilderness but also because verse 13 depicts the servant of God trampling the serpent underfoot. This calls to mind God's curse upon the serpent in Eden (see Genesis 3:15) and Paul's insistence that "the God of peace will soon crush Satan under your feet" at Jesus' return (Romans 16:20).

TRUST THIS TRUTH

The Old Testament offers us the ringing, even singing, affirmation that the Most High rules over all His creation. There is no force influencing our lives that is not answerable to Him.

We might naturally infer from this that the Most High will protect His people from all evil and deliver them from all pain. "If the Most High is good," the thinking might go, "bad things won't happen."

But as we saw in Psalm 91, even the person who loves God, knows His name, and receives promises to be spared from evil might experience trouble. Bad things do happen to good people. Does this mean God is not the Most High or (what is worse) that the Most High is not good?

The Bible presents us with three irrefutable facts: (1) The Jews suffered, (2) Jesus suffered, and (3) the church suffered, yet all of them continued to worship God as the Most High. Somehow, they saw in their sorrow His plan. They did not assume He would always use His power to work out their purposes, and they knew their pain wasn't purposeless.

Perhaps we see this most clearly in the life of our Lord as He suffered anguish in Gethsemane, the garden where He prayed before His arrest. Read Matthew 26:36-46.

18. What state was Jesus in when He withdrew into the garden to pray (see verses 37-38)?

19. The "cup" symbolizes the full measure of God's wrath against sin. With this in mind, how would you restate the request Jesus made in verse 39?

20. Describe any differences you observe between Jesus' prayers in verse 39 and verse 42.

21. Why do you suppose Jesus "went away and prayed for the third time, saying the same words again" (verse 44)?

▶ There's an easily overlooked fact about Jesus' prayer in the Garden of Gethsemane. There was no one awake to listen to what He was saying. Jesus must have thought this time of prayer important enough to relate to the disciples after His resurrection!

---

22. During Jesus' ordeal in Gethsemane, the disciples simply could not stay awake. At His time of greatest need, they offered no support. When He finally roused them to leave the garden, He announced, "Behold, the hour is at hand, and the Son of Man is being betrayed into the hands of sinners" (verse 45, NKJV). How would you describe Jesus' attitude at this point?

23. Consider Jesus' statements later in this chapter, specifically in verses 52-56, alongside His prayer in Gethsemane. What was Jesus certain of at the time He surrendered Himself to His accusers?

24. What is one life lesson about suffering according to God's will that you would draw from Jesus' experience in Gethsemane?

25. How do you think knowing the Father as the Most High affected the way Jesus dealt with this terrible situation?

26. Neither the Scriptures nor the experiences of life give us any good reason to expect that life will be filled with ease and happiness. In fact, both give us reason to expect the opposite. Why then are we so often blindsided and upset when troubles come our way?

27. Write out one sentence below that will help focus your attention on what is true about your Father, the Most High God, in the face of your own troubles.

MEMORIZE THIS MESSAGE

I will be glad and exult in you; I will sing praise to your name, O Most High. (Psalm 9:2)

WORSHIP IN THESE WORDS

As we learned in Psalm 47, God's sovereign rule over all the powers of heaven and earth is something to sing about. Meditate on this hymn in your private devotions. Feel free to read it together at the end of your small-group meeting, with a different person reading each stanza.

"The One God"
Words attributed to Simon Browne

Eternal God! Almighty Cause
Of earth, and seas, and worlds unknown!
All things are subject to Thy laws;
All things depend on Thee alone.

Thy glorious being singly stands,
Of all within itself possessed;
By none controlled in Thy commands,
And in Thyself completely blessed.

Worship to Thee alone belongs,
Worship to Thee alone we give;
Thine be our hearts and Thine our songs,
And to Thy glory may we live.

O, spread Thy truth through every land,
In every heart Thy love be known;
Subdue the world to Thy command,
And, as Thou art, reign God alone.[3]

3

THE MIGHTY ONE

Who Beckons You into the Battles Only He Can Win

Finally, be strong in the Lord and in the strength of his might.

Ephesians 6:10

ROBERT

I got into only one fight during my school days, and it ended almost as quickly as it began. Jimmy was mad at me. I don't remember why, but I had probably insulted him in some way or another. (In fifth grade, I had the sensitivity of a rhinoceros.) Whatever the case, Jimmy was determined to beat me up at recess.

I did my best to avoid the conflict, not because I was a philosophical pacifist or religious peacemaker but because I was skinny and had no idea how to hit someone. The thought of a fist-to-fist fight disconcerted me because I was sure it would end up being fist-to-face—my face.

Alas, Jimmy was not an even-tempered boy, and he was resolved to fight me. We squared up near the merry-go-round, and he began his threats, kind of like Achilles at the walls of Troy, only with less polish. Everyone in the world gathered around to watch the spectacle. Jimmy gave me a shove and watched me stumble backward. It was the last thing he saw for the next sixty-five seconds.

As I tumbled onto my backside, Robert stepped forward and punched Jimmy in the jaw. His glasses went flying over the seesaw, and he had to spend the next minute searching for them. The fight was over.

To this day, I have no idea why Robert stepped in to save me. He was the biggest kid in our class, having served a two-year sentence in fifth grade, and I didn't know him very well. Perhaps he had a beef with Jimmy or simply felt the need to punch someone at recess that day. Whatever the case, I was really grateful that Robert stepped in to help me. I was also grateful that we didn't live in medieval times, because I would have had to swear fealty to a guy who might never see sixth grade.

It was the first and best (albeit bad) example I had of someone stepping in to fight for me. Ever since, I have been fond of the idea of someone keeping near enough to me to fight on my behalf.

God is just such a defender. In the Bible, He is called "the Mighty One" or "the Almighty," a warrior who can close on adversaries and thwart the blows of enemies with total effectiveness. He did it for the Israelites when they left Egypt. Weakened by generations of cruel slavery, they stood no chance of success if Egypt sought to destroy them. Yet the Mighty One rose up to fight for them.

Under similar circumstances later in history, the Mighty One fought for His people by strengthening their hands for the work of rebuilding and defending their capital city, Jerusalem. In both cases, God was near enough and strong enough to stand against the staunchest enemies coming at His people. But is He near to you?

As on my elementary playground, there are times when people and forces array against you, and you know your well-being is at stake. Will God really fight for you? Does He really have *all might*? If the Scriptures say it's so, then be prepared to relate to God as the Mighty One.

THE MIGHTY ONE FIGHTS FOR YOU

Exodus 15:1-13 is part of a song Moses composed to commemorate Israel's deliverance from the Egyptians. For generations, the Israelites had served as slaves in Egypt. Their backs and spirits had been bent to breaking until Moses appeared before Pharaoh with a word from the Lord: "Let my people go" (Exodus 5:1).

After the Lord struck Egypt with ten terrible plagues, Pharaoh finally relented and let Israel go. Though they were "equipped for battle" (Exodus 13:18), they were not mentally ready to encounter warfare (see Exodus 13:17). Warfare, it turned out, was coming to them anyway, for no sooner had Israel reached the outskirts of Egypt than Pharaoh changed his mind and sent chariots and foot soldiers to halt Israel's march. You will not find God addressed as the Mighty One explicitly in this passage, but it records the most outstanding display of God's power to redeem His people from hostile forces. Read Exodus 14:10–15:3.

1. What was the mood in the camp of Israel by the Red Sea (see Exodus 14:10-12)? Why?

2. The Israelites looked at the Egyptians and saw certain doom approaching. To where did Moses direct their attention (see verses 13-14)?

3. Why did God harden Pharaoh's heart and deliver Israel through the Red Sea the way He did (see verses 15-18)?

4. What impression of God do you get from His words in verses 15-18?

5. The Lord directly intervened in this crisis by sending "the angel of God . . . and the pillar of cloud" (verse 19) to stand between Israel and Egypt until all His people had crossed safely to the other side of the sea on dry ground. But when the Egyptians pursued them, the ground was no longer dry, and mud clogged their chariot wheels. At this point, what realization dawned on the Egyptian forces (see verse 25)?

6. The Egyptian hosts had no time to retreat. The wall of water that permitted Israel safe passage collapsed and drowned all in Pharaoh's army. The next morning, Israel looked out over a battleground they had not fought on. What did they recognize about the Lord that morning? How did they respond (see verses 30-31)?

7. Safe on the far shore of the Red Sea, with no enemy behind them, Moses and the people worshipped God. For what attributes did they praise Him (see 15:1-3)?

▶ The song recorded in Exodus 15:1-16 is significant, not only because a hundred generations have learned of God's mighty deliverance through it but because it's part of the playlist in heaven! In the book of Revelation, John gave this account of a scene in heaven: "And I saw what appeared to be a sea of glass mingled with fire — and also those who had conquered . . . And they sing the song of Moses, the servant of God, and the song of the Lamb, saying, 'Great and amazing are your deeds, O Lord God the Almighty! Just and true are your ways, O King of the nations!'" (Revelation 15:2-3).

8. Describe the difference between acknowledging the fact that God is strong and proclaiming that God "is *my* strength . . . *my* song . . . *my* salvation" (Exodus 15:2). How do you make the shift from one to the other?

9. Has God ever fought for you? If so, when? If you think He hasn't, what do you make of that?

THE MIGHTY ONE FIGHTS WITH YOU

When Israel matched up against Egypt during the exodus, God stepped in and punched the adversary out without Israel lifting a finger. "Fear not," Moses had said, and "stand firm . . . the LORD will fight for you, and you have only to be silent" (Exodus 14:13-14).

This would not always be the case.

The Mighty One will fight for us, to be sure. We never fight alone. Yet fight we must, most of the time. The Almighty is more than capable of taking on the powers of this world in single combat, but He generally calls on us to prepare for war and march into battle. We fight with the Mighty One. He rarely fights without us.

▶ In addition to the overthrow of Egypt at the Red Sea, there are only a handful of battles in Israel's history in which no human weapon was taken up to defeat an imposing adversary. One such story is found in 2 Chronicles 20:15-17, where the prophet Jahaziel assured God's people, "Do not be afraid and do not be dismayed at this great horde, for the battle is not yours but God's. . . . *You will not need to fight in this battle.* Stand firm, hold your position, and see the salvation of the LORD on your behalf" (emphasis added). So certain was King Jehoshaphat in this promise that he marched toward the battlefield the next day with the choir in front of the army!

Many centuries after Moses, the Jewish people found themselves banished from their homeland, their capital city of Jerusalem in ruins after a series of devastating attacks. God raised up a man named Nehemiah to leave his government post in the court of Persia and return to Jerusalem to rebuild the ruined wall. (A stout wall ensured stability for a city in the ancient world.)

Nehemiah faced immediate opposition from the nations around Jerusalem. They had grown stronger during the Jewish Exile and were hardly pleased with the momentum Nehemiah brought to the rebuilding effort. Read Nehemiah 4:7-23, which tells the story of that time.

10. What peril did the people in Jerusalem face (see verses 7-8)?

11. How did Nehemiah and the people respond to this threat (see verse 9)?

12. If they trusted God to answer their prayers, why do you suppose they posted guards?

13. In addition to open threat, discouraging messages also undermined the resolve of the rebuilders. Who sent these discouraging messages, and what did they say (see verses 10-12)?

14. Describe the tactical preparations Nehemiah took to prepare the people for assault while continuing work on the wall (see verses 13-20).

15. A distant observer of the rebuilding efforts would have seen a highly organized, heavily armed, and well-guarded operation going on from sunup to sundown. It looked as if the Jews were accomplishing this work through their own grit. But this was hardly the view of Nehemiah and the people. In what ways did they see God supporting them in this conflict (see 4:9,14,20; 6:9)?

16. The book of Nehemiah tells us that the work of rebuilding the wall took only fifty-two days to complete, a feat so impressive that "all the nations around [them] were afraid and fell greatly in their own esteem" (6:16). According to this verse, why were Israel's enemies so affected by their success?

17. God's people were working hard in Nehemiah's day, and they were prepared to fight if it came to it. Nevertheless, they did not believe they were standing alone. What about you? As you "toil and strive" for godliness (1 Timothy 4:10) and "fight the good fight of the faith" (1 Timothy 6:12), do you ever feel like it's all up to you? If so, what gives you that impression?

18. How can you foster a keener awareness of God's part in the battles you face?

_____

▶ "Work as if it all depended upon you. Pray as if it all depended upon God." No one knows who first spoke these words, though some think it might have been St. Augustine. Whether the saying originated in antiquity or not, the idea can be found as far back as 445 BC, when Nehemiah said, "We prayed to our God and set a guard as a protection against [our enemies] day and night" (Nehemiah 4:9).

_____

FACING YOUR ENEMIES WITH THE MIGHTY ONE

It's impossible to fight a battle with an enemy we haven't identified. This doesn't mean we have to see them standing in front of us with fists clenched, as I did on the playground in fifth grade. (Remember Jimmy?) However, we must know the adversaries we are up against if we intend to fight wisely and well.

19. The following passages help us identify the opposition we face today. In each one, underline the powers or people you and the Mighty One will be squaring up against:

When I was with you day after day in the temple, you did not lay hands on me. But this is your hour, and the power of darkness. (Luke 22:53)

You were dead in the trespasses and sins in which you once walked, following the course of this world, following the prince of the power of the air, the spirit that is now at work in the sons of disobedience. (Ephesians 2:1-2)

We do not wrestle against flesh and blood, but against the rulers, against the authorities, against the cosmic powers over this present darkness, against the spiritual forces of evil in the heavenly places. (Ephesians 6:12)

Pray for us, that the word of the Lord may speed ahead and be honored, as happened among you, and that we may be delivered from wicked and evil men. For not all have faith. (2 Thessalonians 3:1-2)

We know that we are from God, and the whole world lies in the power of the evil one. (1 John 5:19)

20. Are you more aware of the danger posed by some of these enemies than others? Which ones?

Which ones are you less aware of?

TRUST THIS TRUTH

As the previous passages make clear, our battles might be invisible, but they are far from abstract. In the same way, people around us might not observe our preparation for battle, but we must be ready to fight or risk defeat. Read Ephesians 6:10-18.

21. In this passage, Paul aimed to make believers battle-ready. What are the first two commands he issued to prepare us for war (see verses 10-11)?

22. What do you think it means to "be strong in the Lord"?

23. Give an example of how you might have to wrestle with "the spiritual forces of evil" (verse 12)?

24. What kind of damage do you suppose these adversaries can do to those of us who believe in Jesus as our Savior and Lord?

25. Four times in four verses (see verses 11-14), Paul urged us to take a stand against the evil one. What are some of the factors in your life that can undermine your resolve to stand against the assaults of Satan?

26. We are enabled to stand in the strength of the Lord as we put on the armor He has made available to us. In what ways does each of the following (from verses 14-17) enable you to stand with the Mighty One as you withstand your adversaries?

• the belt of truth

• the breastplate of righteousness

• shoes that signify the readiness given by the gospel of peace

• the shield of faith

- the helmet of salvation

- the sword of the Spirit

27. Prayer is an essential part of this battle. What do you think it means to pray "in the Spirit" (verse 18)?

28. Choose a battle you are now facing. Why is prayer necessary in this situation?

29. What are some of the alternatives to fighting against our adversaries?

30. Is there anything you will do differently as a result of this study? If so, what?

MEMORIZE THIS MESSAGE

Finally, be strong in the Lord and in the strength of his might. (Ephesians 6:10)

WORSHIP IN THESE WORDS

In your own devotional time or small group discussion, consider singing or reciting the words of this hymn to praise the Mighty One, whose strength and kingdom will never fail and whose Son is victorious over Satan.

"A Mighty Fortress Is Our God"
By Martin Luther

> *A mighty fortress is our God, a bulwark never failing;*
> *Our helper He, amid the flood of mortal ills prevailing:*
> *For still our ancient foe doth seek to work us woe;*
> *His craft and power are great, and, armed with cruel hate,*
> *On earth is not his equal.*
>
> *Did we in our own strength confide, our striving would be losing;*
> *Were not the right Man on our side, the Man of God's own choosing:*
> *Dost ask who that may be? Christ Jesus, it is He;*

Lord Sabaoth,[1] His Name, from age to age the same,
And He must win the battle.

And though this world, with devils filled, should threaten to undo us,
We will not fear, for God hath willed His truth to triumph through us:
The Prince of Darkness grim, we tremble not for him;
His rage we can endure, for lo, his doom is sure,
One little word shall fell him.

That Word above all earthly powers, no thanks to them, abideth;
The Spirit and the gifts are ours through Him Who with us sideth:
Let goods and kindred go, this mortal life also;
The body they may kill: God's truth abideth still,
His kingdom is forever.[2]

4

THE ROCK

Who Provides Us with a Firm Place to Stand

Trust in the LORD forever, for in GOD the LORD, we have an everlasting Rock.
ISAIAH 26:4, NASB

MR. FAILE

Mr. Faile. It was so unlikely. My AP physics class in high school was taught by Mr. Faile.

He loved classical music, tube amps, and experimentation. He was portly, in the not-refined sense of that word, and he frequently wore brown suits. I really liked Mr. Faile, though, but not because he was the most energetic lecturer or the kindest teacher. Rather, he was eccentric, slovenly, and somewhat remote, but he loved physics and his name was Mr. Faile. It was a most improbable combination, the kind you admire just because it is.

Very few of my friends passed the AP physics test at the end of our senior year. After all, our teacher was Mr. Faile. Maybe his name had gotten into our heads. Or maybe his lectures hadn't.

Has the name of God gotten into your head—in a good way? Has it influenced the direction of your life, the substance of your prayers, and the way you speak to others about Him? God is very deliberate about revealing His nature to us through His names. He has even broken out into metaphor to do so.

That is precisely what God did when He told us to call Him "the Rock." Rendering it in Hebrew—*tsoor*—makes it sound more remote, but it doesn't change the meaning. People called God "the Rock" or "my Rock" in the Bible. God even referred to Himself this way, saying, "Is there a God besides me? There is no Rock; I know not any" (Isaiah 44:8).

Of course, this name is a metaphor, a sign pointing to something else. But it isn't an accidental occurrence, like having a physics teacher named Mr. Faile (or a really short first-grade teacher named Mrs. Dolly, by the way). No, it's a strategic revelation of God's nature by way of a name—a very poetic name.

He is the Rock. He did not say He is the Ocean or the Expanse or any other such thing. But He did say He is the Rock. That is fuel for the imagination.

Imagination, however, should never be granted sovereignty over investigation when the Scriptures speak. If God is the Rock, surely He has told us something in the Word about what this name means. If not, one person might think of God as Mount Everest, another as a pebble in a brook, and another as a giant diamond on a rich lady's finger!

The field of possible interpretations narrows somewhat when we open the Bible. There, we discover what the Rock was telling us by His name.

THE ROCK IS RIGHTEOUS IN ALL HIS WAYS

Deuteronomy 32 is a lyrical piece that Moses composed just before his death as the people of Israel camped by the Jordan River and prepared to take possession of the land God had promised them. Curiously, though, at this time of great national expectation Moses wrote out this song as a testimony against Israel for future generations. Read Deuteronomy 32:1-18.

1. Deuteronomy 32:4 is the first time God is referred to as the Rock. What attributes did Moses associate with that name in this verse?

2. How does Israel's response to God contrast with His character (see verses 5-6)?

3. In light of the judgment that Moses foresaw in Israel's future, why would it be important for people to understand and accept these attributes?

4. Lest the people forget God's ways of dealing with them in their early days, Moses said, "Remember the days of old . . . ask your father, and he will show you, your elders, and they will tell you" (verse 7). List three of the ways God had shown grace and mercy to Israel in earlier days (see verses 8-14).

5. In verse 15, the Lord referred to Israel as "Jeshurun," a term of endearment that came from a Hebrew root meaning "upright" or "just" — the very attribute Moses had ascribed to the Rock (see verse 4)! As we discover in verses 15-18, however, God's people had been anything but upright or faithful. Why did they turn away from the Lord?

6. Based on what you've read in these verses, in what respect is God like a rock?

_____

▶ In response to Israel's provocation, God promised to heap misfortune, famine, plague, and bitter destruction on the people (see Deuteronomy 32:23-24), relenting only so that Israel's enemies would not "misunderstand . . . [and] say, 'Our hand is triumphant, it was not the LORD who did all this'" (32:27). In the midst of such calamities, Israel would be tempted to find fault with God and deny the justness of His ways. That is why Moses called people to recognize the Rock's nature in a time of peace. Perhaps, then, future generations would be more willing to hold on to the truth about God's justice in spite of their shifting circumstances and moods.[1]

_____

THE ROCK IS STRONG ON OUR BEHALF

In an age of high-tech warfare, when planes can drop bombs and missiles soar for miles, we seldom reflect on the strategic value a mountain fortress held in ancient times. If you controlled the high ground and enjoyed the natural protection of impenetrable rock, your enemies had to fight more than just you. They had to take on the forces of gravity and granite as well! David, the great warrior-king of Israel, knew this very well, and he employed this image in order to worship and witness to God. Read 2 Samuel 22:1-20.

7. What does verse 1 tell us about the circumstances that gave rise to David's song?

8. List every metaphor David used to describe God in 2 Samuel 22:2-3, and comment on the strategic significance each would have played in battle.

9. When we call on God as the Rock, we should not think of Him as incapable of coming to us when the situation gets dire. (Remember, the Rock is a descriptive name, not just an imaginative metaphor!) How did David represent God's saving activity in 2 Samuel 22:10-18?

▶ The next time you hear someone refer to a well-behaved toddler as "a little cherub," dive for cover into the nearest open room. It might seem a bit dramatic, but you'll be doing your part to salvage an accurate view of angels. Cherubs are not pudgy boy-angels who sit on clouds and shoot lovers with heart-tipped arrows. They are warrior-angels qualified to accompany the Master of the Universe in battle. In 2 Samuel 22:11, David envisioned God mounting a cherub to fly into conflict with the wings of the wind. Try rendering that scene on a Valentine's Day card!

---

10. By His very nature, God offers us the saving protection of a fortress and the spirited help of a warrior. But beyond both of these, He offers us inward, even bodily, strength so we can endure the contests of life. David described this God-given experience in 2 Samuel 22:32-37. Describe a recent experience in which you called on God and experienced the saving strength of the Rock. (If you can't think of such an experience, why do you suppose that's the case?)

11. How should we respond to the difficulties we face in life? Consider the clues that David left in 2 Samuel 22:4,7.

▶ God is referred to as the Rock three times more often in the book of Psalms than in any other book of the Bible. Perhaps the metaphor simply fit the creative needs of "the sweet psalmist of Israel" (2 Samuel 23:1). But maybe there is another explanation. David was not merely a musician; he was a warrior throughout his life. One wonders when he even found time to compose poetry as he was fleeing to the mountains, fighting out of fortresses, or setting up strongholds along the borderlands of Israel. More than any other writer of biblical literature, David was best qualified to grasp and worship God as the Rock because he best understood the role of a "fortress . . . shield . . . and stronghold" (2 Samuel 22:2-3).

THE ROCK WE MUST BELIEVE IN

The Old Testament teaches us to look to the Rock and put our trust in Him if we hope to be saved. "For God alone my soul waits in silence; from him comes my salvation," David wrote. "He alone is my rock and my salvation, my fortress; I shall not be greatly shaken" (Psalm 62:1-2).

Jesus called us to come to Him as the Rock, or Cornerstone, and put our faith in Him. Underscore every instance of the word *rock* or *stone* and circle every instance of the word *believe* in the following passage (1 Peter 2:6-8):

It stands in Scripture:

> *"Behold, I am laying in Zion a stone,*
> *a cornerstone chosen and precious,*
> *and whoever believes in him will not be put to shame." [Isaiah 28:16]*

So the honor is for you who believe, but for those who do not believe,

*"The stone that the builders rejected
has become the cornerstone," [Psalm 118:22]*

and

*"A stone of stumbling,
and a rock of offense." [Isaiah 8:14]*

They stumble because they disobey the word, as they were destined to do.

12. How do you reconcile the contrast Peter drew when he called Jesus both "a cornerstone chosen and precious" and a "stone of stumbling, and a rock of offense"?

13. Before the advent of poured concrete foundations, what role did a cornerstone play in the construction of a building? (If you don't know, an Internet search will probably yield an answer.)

14. Salvation has always come to those who have looked to God, the Rock, for salvation. Conversely, those who have rejected His justice or saving strength have been destroyed. In what respects does Jesus now represent the ultimate display of God's justice and the full offer of His salvation from disaster?

TRUST THIS TRUTH

15. There is a difference between calling God "the Rock" and relying on Him as "my Rock," especially when life is hard. Do you look back on any past disappointments or pain and wonder, "Where was God in all this?" If so, describe one of those painful situations.

16. Meditate and pray about the memory you just described. Use the words of Deuteronomy 32:4, but in this instance personalize the Scripture, saying, "*My* Rock, his work is perfect, for all his ways are justice. A God of faithfulness and without iniquity, just and upright is he."

17. God is our protection, and we can trust Him to defend us. Why then do we often feel the need to protect ourselves?

18. In what areas of life have you been trying to stand your ground in your own strength when you should have been fleeing to your Fortress and allowing God to lead the offensive?

19. When you call on God as the Rock this week, what are three attributes associated with this name that you will call to mind?

MEMORIZE THIS MESSAGE

Trust in the LORD forever, for in GOD the LORD, we have an everlasting Rock. (Isaiah 26:4, NASB)

WORSHIP IN THESE WORDS

How firm a foundation do you stand on? Sometimes the trials of life make it seem like everything is giving way, and we are tempted to question why God permits trouble to come our way. In times like this, we need to listen to the Word of God more than our own imagination. God is a Rock, and His Word can be trusted. These two truths are affirmed in the hymn "How Firm a Foundation."

The first verse of this hymn forms an introduction, an affirmation that all who have sought refuge in Jesus can trust fully in God's promises. The subsequent stanzas are based on scriptural promises God has made to guard and guide those who are His own. Let the first stanza challenge you to trust in God as the Rock and the subsequent verses encourage you with His promises!

"How Firm a Foundation"
By John Rippon

How firm a foundation, ye saints of the Lord,
Is laid for your faith in His excellent Word!
What more can He say than to you He hath said,
To you who for refuge to Jesus have fled?

Fear not, I am with thee, O be not dismayed,
For I am thy God and will still give thee aid;
I'll strengthen and help thee, and cause thee to stand
Upheld by My righteous, omnipotent hand.

When through fiery trials thy pathway shall lie,
My grace, all sufficient, shall be thy supply;
The flame shall not hurt thee; I only design
Thy dross to consume, and thy gold to refine.

The soul that on Jesus has leaned for repose,
I will not, I will not desert to its foes;
That soul, though all hell should endeavor to shake,
I'll never, no never, no never forsake.[2]

5

THE JEALOUS ONE

Who Demands Total Loyalty and Offers Steadfast Love

You shall worship no other god, for the LORD, whose name is Jealous, is a jealous God.

EXODUS 34:14

RIVALRY

There is a state down South where the war hasn't ended. I'm not talking about the Civil War, but the contest between two rival schools: Auburn University and the University of Alabama.

If you haven't lived in Alabama and measured the strength of this rivalry, you only need to find someone who has. Or better yet, go to the Iron Bowl next Thanksgiving weekend and see for yourself.

Haven't you heard of the Iron Bowl? It's the annual contest between the Auburn and Alabama football teams. It is easier to find tickets to the president's inauguration than to find tickets to this game.

In the state of Alabama, it's hard to remain neutral on the question of these rivals. Do you cheer for Auburn or Alabama? It can't be both. If you grew up wearing crimson and white, you cannot bear the sight of orange and blue. If you follow the Auburn Tigers, you cannot bear to hear the cheer "Roll Tide." It wouldn't surprise me if the Alabama Health Department made parents declare for one of the two schools on behalf of their children when they're born.

In fact, so deep-seated is the contention between these schools that if I indicated which one I attended, I would immediately alienate the portion of my audience that attended the other.

(War Eagle.)

If you attended a college with lots of school spirit and an in-state rivalry, chances are you understand something about the way loyalty makes associations with rivals unthinkable. But university spirit is only a gateway into another, stronger attachment that will carry us further toward an understanding of God's jealousy.

The best analogy we have of the divine jealousy is human marriage, not because jealousy invariably goes right in marriage but because it is appropriate when it doesn't go wrong. Spouses often do and always should love one another with a fierce, ardent love that allows no competition. Partners should never permit a rival affection to arise in their hearts, and they do not rest if they suspect one has arisen in their spouse's. Husbands do not approve of their wives sleeping with a few other men. Wives do not tolerate their husbands having a tryst or two per decade.

The love of a husband for a wife is a jealous love. *It ought to be this way.* Both partners ought to feel the strongest sense of devotion to one another and behave accordingly.

In marriage, the loyalty and love accompanying proper jealousy are fires that warm. The ardor and bond of love is one of the greatest blessings on earth. Yet jealousy is also a fire that can scorch when affection and trust are trampled by infidelity. Marriage helps us understand how the same fire that comforts and protects might flare and destroy. The love of a husband and wife lifts our gaze as high as human relationships can take us toward heaven.

But it is not high enough. There is a higher, holier love in heaven, and the jealousy of our God should not be overlooked. In fact, it cannot be, because we must address Him as the Jealous One if we are to call Him by name.

TEN COMMANDMENTS FROM THE JEALOUS ONE

1. *Jealousy* is a word loaded with negative associations. We need to cast a lot of these overboard as we try to understand God's holy jealousy. In the space below, list every attribute of human jealousy you think is inapplicable to or unworthy of God.

▶ "The English [word] 'jealousy' derives from Gk. *zelos*, the same root from which the English 'zeal' derives. The Hebrew and Greek vocabularies do not distinguish, as modern English does, between these two intense emotions. In the English versions, only the context determines whether Heb. *qin'a* and Gk. *zelos* are to be translated as 'zeal' or 'jealousy.'"[1]

God's jealousy is not an unholy or unhealthy thing like human self-centeredness. In fact, it's not just a characteristic but an attribute of God so near to Him that we may properly address Him by name as "Jealous" or "the Jealous One." Nowhere do we see God's jealousy more clearly on display than in the Ten Commandments. Read Exodus 20:1-21.

2. What do the following commandments contribute to our understanding of God's jealousy?

You shall have no other gods before me. (Exodus 20:3)

*You shall not make for yourself a carved image, or any likeness of anything that is in heaven above, or that is in the earth beneath, or that is in the water under the earth. You shall not bow down to them or serve them, for I the L*ORD *your God am a jealous God. (Exodus 20:4-5)*

*You shall not take the name of the L*ORD *your God in vain, for the L*ORD *will not hold him guiltless who takes his name in vain. (Exodus 20:7)*

*Remember the Sabbath day, to keep it holy. . . . For in six days the L*ORD *made heaven and earth, the sea, and all that is in them, and rested on the seventh day. Therefore the L*ORD *blessed the Sabbath day and made it holy. (Exodus 20:8,11)*

3. In chapter 1 on "the Holy One," we studied Exodus 19, the chapter that precedes the Ten Commandments. In what ways do you think an accurate understanding of God's holiness helps us make sense of His jealousy?

4. What kind of response do we rouse in God when we disregard His will (see Exodus 20:5-6)?

What about when we obey?

_____

▶ Through the Ten Commandments, God issued a warning that He would visit "the iniquity of the fathers on the children to the third and the fourth generation of those who hate [him]" (Exodus 20:5). Does this mean children will be held guilty for their parents' sins? Deuteronomy 24:16 suggests this would be an injustice. Children will not share in their parents' *guilt* before God; however, they will suffer the *consequences* of their parents' sins.

_____

5. Time and again, God warned Israel not to succumb to the idolatrous practices of the nations around them. He repeatedly commanded them to destroy the idols and sanctuaries where false gods were worshipped in the Promised Land. Later in Exodus,

God commanded, "You shall tear down their altars and break their pillars and cut down their Asherim (for you shall worship no other god, for the LORD, *whose name is Jealous*, is a jealous God)" (Exodus 34:13-14, emphasis added). We know God was not threatened by idols. Why, then, do you think their presence in Israel was such an affront to Him?

6. At the foot of Mount Sinai, in the midst of "thunder and the flashes of lightning" (Exodus 20:18), the people of Israel had a strong incentive to follow God. Yet Moses continued to warn them not to defect from the Lord to serve other gods (see, for instance, Deuteronomy 6:10-15). Why do you think these repeated warnings were necessary?

7. What are some of the things you're tempted to treat as a higher priority than God? These might be things you sometimes desire more than you desire God or things you sometimes fear more than you trust God. (Our use of money and time sometimes points out where we are serving false gods.)

NO ROOM FOR FALSE WORSHIP

The Lord did not urge His people to honor Him simply with commands and warnings. He also gave them examples so they could see in their own history how His demand for utter loyalty and commitment to steadfast love manifested itself.

When Moses ascended Mount Sinai to receive the Law from God, he left the people of Israel behind for more than a month (see Exodus 24:18). After such a long delay, the people approached Aaron, the high priest, and demanded, "Up, make us gods who shall go before us!" (Exodus 32:1). The Hebrew word translated as "gods" in this verse is the same one frequently used in the Old Testament for the one true God—*elohim*. (For instance, *elohim* is the word translated as "God" throughout Genesis 1.) It's unlikely the people were turning to polytheism in this moment; rather, they were asking for a visible idol to represent their unseen *elohim*, who had called them out of Egypt. (See sidebar on page 78.)

Read Exodus 32:1-14.

8. Why do you suppose the people asked Aaron to make them an image of god (or gods, per the Hebrew *elohim*) to go before them (see verse 1)?

9. What does it say about the human heart that God's people would abandon the first of the Ten Commandments so soon after they had vowed to follow them?

10. Why should God have been opposed to His people making a golden statue to represent Him if it was truly Him they sought to worship?

▶ "It must . . . be granted that Aaron does not appear to have . . . designed a worship that should supersede the worship of The Most High; hence we find him making proclamation, 'Tomorrow is a feast to the LORD'; and we find farther that some of the proper rites of the true worship were observed on this occasion, for they brought burnt-offerings and peace-offerings (see Ex. 32:6, 7): hence, it is evident he intended that the true God should be the object of their worship, though he permitted and even encouraged them to offer this worship through an idolatrous medium, the molten calf."[2]

---

11. It would be fair to say that ever since God created humanity in His image, humanity has been trying to repay the favor. There's something convenient about making a god in your own image. The gods we make are easier to live with because they suit our preferences—like ordering coffee or a burger just the way you like it. If you were left to create a god in your own image, how would that god look and act? Like a benevolent Santa Claus? A patriotic American? A strict moralist?

What's wrong with doing that?

12. How is the worship around the golden calf described in Exodus 32:5-6?

13. While the people of Israel were fashioning an *elohim* to worship in the valley, Moses remained on the mountain, receiving more laws from God with which to govern His people. Eventually, though, God alerted Moses to the problem. What wrongs did God accuse Israel of in Exodus 32:7-9?

14. Exodus 32:10 begins with the Lord saying to Moses, "Now therefore let me alone . . ." This suggests that Moses had already begun to intercede for the Israelites as soon as he heard about their treachery. It's ridiculous to suppose Moses could have prevented God from destroying Israel if God had settled this purpose in His heart. (In a later passage, Deuteronomy 10:10, Moses actually

declared, "The LORD was unwilling to destroy you.") Rather, God seemed to be testing Moses by offering to build a nation through his descendants and leaving it in Moses' hands to decide. Moses passed this test by continuing to intercede for Israel in verses 11-13. Upon what bases did he make his appeal to God to spare Israel?

As the chapter concludes, we learn that many people involved in this "great sin" (32:21) were executed or killed in a plague. However, the camp of Israel included more than six hundred thousand men plus women and children at this point (see Exodus 12:37-38). A vast majority of the people were brought under conviction but not into judgment for their sin. Through His severity and mercy, God demonstrated His jealousy to His people and for His people, His demand for loyalty, and His offer of steadfast love.

GOD'S JEALOUSY AND OUR GOOD

Because God is the Jealous One, we know we should be devoted to Him. Seldom do we consider, however, that His jealousy disposes Him to show us love and affection. Human jealousy might lapse into selfishness, but God's will always inclines Him toward generosity. He is as jealous for our well-being as He is for our worship. In fact, He aims to secure our well-being by calling us to undivided worship, for setting our hearts on God means setting our hearts on the highest good we can attain.

▶ What's the difference between jealousy and envy? We often use the two words as synonyms. The distinction is significant, though: I might be envious of what you have, but I am jealous of you. One has to do with possessions, the other of persons. If we knew nothing else of God besides the bare fact that His name is the Jealous One, we would know He is interested and involved in intense, personal relationships.

It is vital to see God's abundant grace in all this, though. He didn't pick through the broken pieces of humanity to find the people with the greatest potential or noblest intentions in order to confer salvation on them. He didn't give us Ten Commandments and say, "I'm a jealous God, and I won't even think about entering into a relationship with you unless you obey at least seven of them." Rather, He sent His one and only Son to die on the cross to redeem people like us. Read Romans 5:6-11.

15. In this passage, what words were used to describe those for whom Jesus died (see verses 6,8,10)?

16. If God saved us when we were ill-deserving, what does this say about His jealous love for us now?

17. J. B. Phillips, in his paraphrase of the New Testament, rendered the meaning of Romans 5:7-8 as follows: "In human experience it is a rare thing for one man to give his life for another, even if the latter be a good man, though there have been a few who have had the courage to do it. Yet the proof of God's amazing love is this: that it was while we were sinners that Christ died for us." Paul added to this foundation several assurances we have in Christ. List three of them from Romans 5:9-11.

18. Shame over past sins can set up a small dominion in our hearts and tell us we're unworthy of God's love until we clean up our act. But God didn't wait for us to straighten ourselves up before He showed us mercy. Rather, "*while* we were still weak . . . *while* we were still sinners . . . *while* we were enemies we were reconciled to God by the death of his Son" (Romans 5:6,8,10, emphasis added). Timing is everything here. In light of this truth, how might you counsel yourself or a friend who feels shut out of God's grace because of past sins?

TRUST THIS TRUTH

Did you wince when you saw a chapter on "the Jealous One" in this book? Did you wonder how someone could massage this concept enough to make it worthy of God? Or did you exclaim, "Another chance to hear the *good news* about how God is for us!"? We seldom think of jealousy as good news because we rarely think of God as the Jealous One. But this is the message of the gospel. The One who has chosen us will not let us go! Paul stressed this point in Romans 8:31-39.

19. Turn the rhetorical questions of Romans 8:31-35 into statements about God's commitment to you in Christ. (Feel free to modify the words used since you are not trying to rewrite the passage but to accept its meaning and implications for your life.)

20. The evidence of God's relentless love for believers is not found in our circumstances—Christians will experience "tribulation . . . distress . . . persecution . . . famine . . . nakedness . . . danger . . . [and] sword" (verse 35). If we're not to look to these circumstances for evidence of God's steadfast love, where should we look?

21. Nothing can separate you from the love of God in Christ. But things like hardship, trouble, and want can provoke you to *feel* like God has forgotten you. At times like these, your faith is tested, for faith is "the art of holding on to things your reason has once accepted, in spite of your changing moods."[3] How might your faith be strengthened during such a trial by addressing God in prayer as the Jealous One?

22. Perhaps our greatest temptation to abandon our devotion to the Jealous One comes during times of ease, not of trial. With so many pleasant possibilities around us, our hearts often turn away from the greatest good, knowing and serving God with a whole heart. We find satisfaction in earthly things and offer God half a heart instead. But is He satisfied with this offering? Does He sit by and smile weakly while we pour our affection and energies out on other unworthy things? Based on the passages we have studied, how do you think God responds when we turn our affection from Him to lesser things?

23. Take some time in prayer to reaffirm your commitment to offer all and withhold none of the following from God:

- Your affection
- Your time
- Your money and possessions
- Your ambitions for the future

MEMORIZE THIS MESSAGE

You shall worship no other god, for the LORD, whose name is Jealous, is a jealous God. (Exodus 34:14)

WORSHIP IN THESE WORDS

Unless you have a private collection of John Wesley's tracts or a copy of his collected works, there is little chance you have seen or sung the untitled hymn below. It was included in a pamphlet Wesley published to encourage Protestant believers to greater personal piety during a Stuart uprising in Scotland. We may only conjecture that John (or possibly his brother Charles) Wesley wrote it.

"Hymn 2" had no accompanying tune. It was, instead, a meditation in meter, a poem meant to arouse true devotion and challenge half-hearted commitment. Pay particular attention to the point that idolatry need not involve *outward ceremony* but *inward attachment* to things like "pleasure, wealth, and fame."

The hymn is really a prayer that the Jealous One might deal mercifully with us and help us deal with the idolatry in our hearts. In this spirit, meditate on the message and recite these words in your private prayer and small-group gathering.

"Hymn 2"
Attributed to John Wesley

Forgive me, O thou jealous God,
A wretch who on thy laws have trod,
    And robbed thee of thy right.
A sinner to myself unknown,
'Gainst thee I have transgress'd, and done
    This evil in thy sight.

My body I disdain'd to incline,
Or worship at an idol's shrine,
        With gross idolatry;
But O! my soul hath baser proved,
Honor'd, and fear'd, and served, and loved
        The creature more than thee.

Let the blind sons of earth[4] bow down,
To images of wood and stone;
        But I with subtler art,
Safe from the letter of thy word,
My idols secretly adored,
        Set up within my heart.

But O! suffice the season past;
My idols now I cast away,
        Pleasure, and wealth, and fame;
The world, and all its goods, I leave,
To thee alone resolved to give,
        Whate'er I have or am.

Lo! in thankful, loving heart,
I render thee whate'er thou art,
        I give myself to thee;
And thee my whole delight I own,
My joy, my glory, and my crown,
        To all eternity. [5]

THE LORD

Who Rightfully Rules Over Us

Why do you call me "Lord, Lord," and not do what I tell you?

LUKE 6:46

"TELL THEM THANKS"

Working in campus ministry, my wife and I see students come and go a lot. Some come once, and you never see them again. Some come often, and you think they'll never leave. The best, however, is when they come in droves to your house and stay up later than you do!

There's nothing like piling a mixed bag of college students—men and women, freshmen and seniors—into a relatively inauspicious house in a quiet neighborhood several miles from campus. It's especially fun at the beginning of a school year when you don't know who most of the students are!

One particular night, students from the University of Wisconsin-Eau Claire, most of them freshmen, had come to our house to eat dinner, play games, and hang out. School had just begun, and we were trying to provide a constructive place for incoming students to spend a Friday night. Better our house than the bars on Water Street.

Several pounds of pizza and innumerable rounds of Spoons (a card game) later, I was beginning to get tired. Never one to be the party pooper, I simply told the remaining students to lock our front door when they decided to leave.

One group took this as a subtle cue to get out, and a carload headed for the door. I accompanied them and bade everyone good night as they left. The last guy stopped at the door, grabbed my hand, and said, "Hey, man, tell your parents thanks for letting us come over!"

Struck dumb, I managed only to mutter, "Okay, I will," as the young man bounded toward the driveway.

I closed the door, the door of *my house*, and positively shook with laughter. What would my mom and dad say the next morning when I called to say thanks for letting fifty freshmen come hang out at my house?

It is said that a man's home is his castle. Apparently, I need to work on my kingly look.

You see, this student had spent an entire evening enjoying the hospitality of our home without ever knowing to whom it belonged. Far from ungrateful, he was one of the few people who took the initiative to say thanks. He just said it to the wrong owner, or to the right owner but . . . not.

So it is with the Lord—*Adonai*, they called him in Hebrew—a name that means "lord," "ruler," "master," or "owner." This name signifies that God is the possessor of all things and the ruler of all people. We should all render thanks to Him today and know that we will all give account to Him someday.[1]

THE RULER OF NATIONS

As we discovered in our chapter on the Most High, God was worshipped from earliest days as the "Possessor of heaven and earth" (Genesis 14:22). In another place we read, "The earth is the LORD's and the fullness thereof, the world and those who dwell therein" (Psalm 24:1). Never was the God of Israel thought to be the god of Israel only. His government, it was believed, extended to all nations.

This belief became increasingly important to Israel as God led them out of Egypt toward the Promised Land. The land had been promised to Israel not because God was able to drive out the lesser gods whose people possessed it but because God was the rightful owner of Canaan and could apportion it to whomever He chose.

Of course, Israel had to trust that God possessed not only the will and the land but the power to deliver it into their hands. An earlier generation of Israelites had walked up to the border of Canaan and quailed at the thought of taking it. When we pick up the story in Joshua, a new generation is standing on the bank of the Jordan River facing the Promised Land. Will they trust the Lord, as their parents failed to do, and go in to take the land? Read Joshua 3:1-17.

1. List as many names for God as you can identify in this chapter.

2. God is identified as *Adon* (a shortened form of *Adonai*, "the Lord") twice in this chapter (see verses 11,13). Over what or whom did God exercise authority in this passage?

Why is this significant?

▶ Genesis 15:2 is the first time Abraham addressed God directly. The
first name he used was *Adonai.*

3. On the day they set out to enter the Promised Land, Israel saw
   what kind of power the Lord wielded over nature. The Jordan
   River, with its strong currents and overflowing banks, "stood and
   rose up in a heap very far away" (Joshua 3:16). Most of the people
   crossing the Jordan at this time were not old enough to remember
   Israel's crossing the Red Sea on their way out of Egypt. How might
   this demonstration of the Lord's power have affected them as they
   prepared for a military campaign in Canaan?

4. The whole nation of Israel—at least six hundred thousand men
   (see Exodus 12:37)—had been camping on the eastern bank of
   the Jordan River just opposite the fortified city of Jericho, which
   lay less than ten miles from the western bank. No doubt, the
   people of Jericho considered a swollen and swift Jordan a good
   defense against invasion by such a large host of people. What
   impression do you think the miracle at the Jordan River left on
   the inhabitants of Jericho when Israel crossed over? (For some
   background on the mood of the people in Jericho prior to this
   miracle, see the comments of a resident of that city recorded in
   Joshua 2:8-11.)

5. Why is it significant for us today to acknowledge the Lord's rightful rule over all the nations of the earth?

6. If the Lord is the rightful ruler over all the nations of the world, how should that affect our view of global events?

How should it affect our day-to-day life?

THE MASTER OF SERVANTS

Adonai is derived from a Hebrew term, *adon*, meaning "lord" or "sir." Kings of Israel were often addressed as "my lord the king," and no king was more deserving of this honorific title than David. That's why it's interesting to note how such a great lord among men spoke to the Lord of all men. Read 2 Samuel 7:16-29.

7. How would you describe David's response to the Lord's promise that he would always have a descendant reigning over Israel (see verses 18-19)?

8. Did David believe that the blessing of God had come to him because of his own merit? If not, then why had it come (see verses 20-21)?

9. The Scriptures leave us in no doubt that David's subjects addressed him as "lord." Perhaps he heard it every day, yet he didn't let an honorific title go to his head. How did David identify himself throughout this passage of Scripture? What does this signify about his attitude?

10. David referred to God as *Adonai*—Lord, Master. He called himself "your servant" ten times in this passage. What responsibility does a servant have to his master?

A master to his servants?

11. Jesus often taught his disciples by telling stories about servants. Read one of the three parables below, and write down any insights you discover about the master-servant relationship in the kingdom of God.

   • Luke 12:35-40
   • Luke 17:7-10
   • Luke 19:11-27

12. What are some of the key resources and responsibilities the Lord has entrusted to you during this season of your life?

THE LORD JESUS CHRIST

When Jesus walked on earth, men called Him "lord." Only the context of their comments can tell us whether they meant to honor Jesus as a great teacher or worship Him as the true Son of God. Jesus pressed this very point to call people into greater commitment to Himself. Read Luke 6:46-49.

13. What kind of behavior did Jesus ask of those who called Him "Lord, Lord"?

▶ "To an early Christian accustomed to reading the OT [Old Testament], the word 'Lord,' when used of Jesus, would suggest his identification with the God of the OT. It expressed Christ's divinity without explicitly asserting his deity, which was an idea startling to non-Christian Jews."[2]

---

14. Why do you think He doubled up the expression "Lord, Lord"? How do you interpret the significance of this expression?

15. Based on this passage, finish the following sentence: "Someone who calls Jesus 'Lord' will . . ."

16. What are the consequences of calling Jesus "Lord" but ignoring His demands?

As we see in Luke 6:46-49, Jesus didn't simply want people to honor Him with a conventional title but to obey Him as God. The disciples carried this message into the whole world as they proclaimed the gospel. The earliest common confession of the Christian church was simply this: "Jesus is Lord" (1 Corinthians 12:3; see also Romans 10:9 and Philippians 2:11).

▶ Most commentators believe that Philippians 2:6-11 is an early Christian hymn that Paul incorporated into one of his letters. If that is the case, then the Christian church has been singing about Jesus' lordship from its earliest days. To say "Jesus is Lord" was a shocking statement in those days because the prevailing oath of allegiance was "Caesar is Lord." Christians were saying that their highest allegiance was to Jesus, not the emperor, and that they would act accordingly.

TRUST THIS TRUTH

When ancient Jews referred to God as *Adonai*, they were calling Him "my Lord" or, more strictly, "my Lords." (The noun appears as first-person, plural, and possessive.) The possessive form suggests a personal identification with God, while the plural form conveys the idea of God's majesty (not multiplicity).

If you look in your Bible, however, you will find that *Adonai* is invariably translated as "the Lord," not "my Lords." Why? It is because the word is not primarily a descriptor but a proper name for God. We call Him the Lord to signify His rightful rule over us.

However, we might benefit from considering the original, personal construction of this word. Perhaps we stand to gain greater insight and deeper trust by acknowledging the grammar God used to reveal Himself to us.

17. What difference does it make to you if you address God as "my Lord" versus "the Lord"?

18. In calling Him "the Lord," we recognize God's grand ownership and mastery over *all* things. But do we actually yield Him control over *our* things? In what areas of your life have you found it difficult to allow the Lord to call the shots and rule over your time, resources, desires, and habits?

19. Which synonyms help you best understand what it means to call on God as your Lord?

    ☐ Master
    ☐ Ruler
    ☐ Owner
    ☐ Other:

    What is it about those synonyms that helps you?

MEMORIZE THIS MESSAGE

Why do you call me "Lord, Lord," and not do what I tell you? (Luke 6:46)

WORSHIP IN THESE WORDS

Philippians 2:10-11 declares that someday "at the name of Jesus every knee [shall] bow, in heaven and on earth and under the earth, and every tongue confess that Jesus Christ is Lord, to the glory of God the Father." One day, all people will acknowledge that Jesus is Lord, regardless of whether they would choose for it to be this way. Those who trust Jesus as Savior now can eagerly anticipate that day of glorious submission and worship Him freely as Lord of all.

If you know the hymn "All Hail the Power of Jesus' Name," use it in your devotional times this week. During your small group meeting, you can read the full text of the hymn aloud or join in singing it together if someone knows the tune.

"All Hail The Power of Jesus' Name"
By Edward Perronet

> *All hail the power of Jesus' name!*
> *Let angels prostrate fall;*
> *Bring forth the royal diadem,*
> *And crown Him Lord of all;*
> *Bring forth the royal diadem,*
> *And crown Him Lord of all!*
>
> *Ye chosen seed of Israel's race,*
> *Ye ransomed from the fall,*
> *Hail Him who saves you by His grace,*
> *And crown Him Lord of all;*
> *Hail Him who saves you by His grace,*
> *And crown Him Lord of all! . . .*

Let every kindred, every tribe,
On this terrestrial ball,
To Him all majesty ascribe,
And crown Him Lord of all;
To Him all majesty ascribe,
And crown Him Lord of all!

O that with yonder sacred throng
We at His feet may fall!
We'll join the everlasting song,
And crown Him Lord of all;
We'll join the everlasting song,
And crown Him Lord of all! [3]

7

THE FATHER

Who Receives Us as Children in His Son

You have received the Spirit of adoption as sons, by whom we cry, "Abba! Father!" The Spirit himself bears witness with our spirit that we are children of God.

Romans 8:15-16

FROM "NORMAN" TO "DADDY"

Until I was twenty-four years old, everyone in the world called me Norman (except for a brief, twenty-four-hour period when some called me Wes—see the introduction). Sure, I had an uncle who called me Stein and a cousin who called me Ragged for reasons none of us can remember, but I went by Norman or Norm just about everywhere I went.

Then I turned twenty-four, and one person started calling me by the name that changed my life forever. My firstborn son started calling me Daddy. Of course, my wife and I have it all chronicled in his baby book. Daddy wasn't his first word. He had to warm up on words like Momma, Lady (our black lab), and "poo poo" before he felt ready for Daddy, but after a few weeks of near constant coaching, he was ready and I became Daddy.

To the wide world I will evermore be Norman. To four children in it, I will always be Daddy.

In actual fact, the kids finessed this name a bit. My oldest son now calls me Dad; my oldest daughter, Daddy; my youngest daughter often calls me D; and my youngest son draws out the first syllable to "Daaa-dee." The discerning reader, however, will see a thread running through all these appellations.

As a fourteen-year veteran of campus ministry, I know many young men who are like sons to me. I have talked with them about schoolwork and sex, drugs and dating, spiritual disciplines and spiritual disappointments, just as I have (or will) with my own children. I have watched these students graduate, get married, and begin their careers. I check in on them periodically to see how their lives are changing. They are like children to me.

But my own children are not *like* children to me. They *are* my kids, and I am their father.

Fatherhood is more than just a responsibility to counsel and nurture young people into adulthood; it's an indissoluble bond God established between a daddy and his kids. It's what defines the gap between being Norman and being Daddy.

With this principle in view, we are ready to take up a vital question in the Bible: Is God *like a father* to us, or is He indeed our Father? The way we answer this question will shape the way we trust in God and talk to Him, and it will influence the way we talk to others about Him. Yet the answers to this question cannot be found or weighed apart from Scripture.

We cannot look within our own heart to know whether God is our Father, for the question, not the answer, lies in our heart. We cannot look to our experiences in this world, for the world is a distortion of what ought to be, and the father-child relationship is often one of the most distorted pictures we have.

No, we have to look to the Scriptures, the record of God's revelation through the prophets and through His Son. There we begin to hear a rumor that the eternal God is eternally a Father—our Father.

If that is true, it changes everything.

GOD IS THE FATHER OF US ALL

As you look around the globe today, what captures your attention? The diversity of human culture or the unity of humankind? Whether in the news or the neighborhood, we are confronted with this tension all the time. Humans are fundamentally the same while fantastically diverse. But where does it all come from?

Modern science, or modern materialism, to be precise, offers a very unsatisfying and barely credible explanation. Presumably, *Homo sapiens* is the only species on the planet capable of developing diverse languages, arts, and habitations while still being accounted the same species.

Without delving further into this debate, suffice it to say there is another, better explanation of human origins, and one need not appeal to the Bible to find it. The apostle Paul certainly didn't when he was in Athens, Greece, and was asked to defend his beliefs about Jesus' resurrection. Read Acts 17:24-31.

1. In verse 28, Paul cited Epimenides and Aratus, two pagan poets known to the cultured Athenians. What two claims did these poets make that Paul agreed with?

2. In what sense are all of us God's children?

3. For some people today, the universal fatherhood of God is a *terminal* point of religious belief. It is enough for some to say, "We are all one, since we all come from the same source." For Paul, however, this assertion was simply a *starting* point. What arguments did he develop from this opening assertion (see verses 29-31)?

4. For other people today, the universal fatherhood of God is denied outright. "There is no evidence for a Creator," the argument might run. Do you think it is necessary today to establish belief in a Supreme Being who created all humanity before introducing someone to the gospel of Jesus Christ? Why or why not?

5. Based on Acts 17:24-31, finish this statement to a non-Christian friend who agrees that one God probably created us all: "Because one God is the Father of us all, each of us must . . ."

THE FATHER OF ISRAEL'S ANOINTED ONE

While there was broad consensus in the ancient world that a Supreme Being created the whole world, the Jewish people had a more refined belief about God's fatherhood. Though they rarely addressed God as "Father," they spoke of the nation of Israel as God's "son" (see, for example, Exodus 4:22 and Hosea 11:1). In displays of tenderness and discipline, God showed that He would deal with His people "as a father the son in whom he delights" (Proverbs 3:12).

But it's one thing to say God is *like* a father and another to say God *is* a father. This is the claim God made when He talked about Israel's king and foreshadowed the coming of the Messiah. In the Old Testament, the anointed one (Hebrew *mashiach*, from which we derive the title Messiah) usually referred to the king of Israel, but the term often foreshadowed the coming of Jesus, who would rule as David's heir over God's people and the nations. Read Psalm 2.

6. Psalm 2 opens by describing the hostility of the nations against the Lord and His anointed king. How did the Lord respond to their open defiance (see verses 4-6)?

7. There is good reason to believe this psalm was composed to celebrate or commemorate the coronation of a new king in Israel. In verses 7-9, the king described the relationship he entered into with the Lord upon his installation. How is their relationship described (see verse 7)?

▶ Are we justified in seeing Jesus, the Messiah, foreshadowed in Psalm 2? The New Testament writers certainly did. In Acts 13:32-33, Paul said, "We bring you the good news that what God promised to the fathers, this he has fulfilled to us their children by raising Jesus, as also it is written in *the second Psalm*, 'You are my Son, today I have begotten you'" (emphasis added).

8. Describe the nature and extent of the Anointed One's dominion (see verses 8-9).

9. How are the nations commanded to relate to the Lord in light of the anointed king's rule (see verses 10-12)?

10. What difference does it make to you that the Messiah (Anointed One) was more than a ruler but also a Son to the Father who sent Him?

▶ In the early centuries of the church, it became important to define with some precision the relation of Jesus the Son to God the Father. At the council of Nicaea in AD 325 (and later at Constantinople in 381), church leaders borrowed from Psalm 2:7 and John 3:16 to affirm that Jesus was "the only-*begotten* Son of God, *begotten* of the Father before all worlds; God of God, Light of Light, very God of very God; *begotten*, not made, being of one substance with the Father, by whom all things were made."[1] Only the One who is begotten shares the same nature with the One who begets. (We seldom use the verb "to beget" these days, but it basically means "to father a child.")

GOD, THE FATHER OF JESUS THE SON

It might seem unnecessary to stress the Father-Son relationship that Jesus shared with God, but the frequency and directness with which Jesus talked about His relationship with His Father is so startling you cannot ignore it. No one had ever walked on earth and said the things Jesus did about the Father. Read John 14:6-14.

11. What role does Jesus play in introducing people into a relationship with the Father (see verses 6-7)?

▶ "The most distinctive development in the use of divine names in the NT [New Testament] is the introduction of the name *Father*. While the idea of 'God as Father' was foreshadowed in the OT [Old Testament] . . . it remained for our Lord to make the usage concrete and intimate."[2]

12. What relation did Jesus bear to the Father (see verses 8-10)?

13. Knowing that His claims were loftier than any person had ever made, Jesus offered His disciples a way to measure whether they were true. What was it (see verse 11)?

14. What difference do Jesus' claims about His relationship to the Father make to the way we pray (see verses 12-14)?

GOD, THE FATHER OF ALL WHO BELIEVE IN THE SON

It is one thing for the Messiah to talk about God as His Father, but Jesus did not stop there. He told His disciples that "he who loves me will be loved by my Father . . . and we will come to him and make our home with him" (John 14:21,23).

So intimate is the relation between God the Father and the Christian believer that Jesus means for us to reinforce the connection every time we pray. Read Luke 11:1-4.

▶ The Lord's Prayer in Luke 11:2-4 differs from the one recorded in Matthew 6:9-13. From this, we can surmise that Jesus taught His disciples to pray using this model on more than one occasion. Matthew's prayer lends itself to corporate praying, and it is the one most often repeated in churches. Luke's version is more personal — not "Our Father" but simply "Father" — it arises from Jesus' concern that His friends learn to pray privately as He did. Because the form of this prayer has come to us with slight variations, we should receive it as Jesus intended: a model prayer to adopt and adapt in public and private worship, not a rote prayer to be recited once a week without thinking.

---

15. What prompted the disciples to say to Jesus, "Lord, teach us to pray" (see verse 1)?

16. The first three phrases of the Lord's Prayer focus primarily on God (see verse 2). Why is each important in shaping the way we pray? (What would we lose if we neglected one of them?)

17. It is significant to see how consistently Jesus practiced what He preached . . . or prayed. When He rejoiced at the disciples' successful ministry, Jesus addressed God as Father (see Luke 10:21). When He prayed about the horrible fate that awaited Him at the cross, He addressed God as Father (see Luke 22:42). Even as the spikes were driven into His hands and feet, Jesus prayed for His enemies, saying, "Father, forgive them, for they know not what they do" (Luke 23:34). How might it shape your prayers in pain, as well as joy, to call on God as your Father?

18. The final three phrases of the Lord's Prayer rest on the foundation of the first three. How does the name Father influence the way you pray these final requests (see 11:3-4)?

TRUST THIS TRUTH

Having given the disciples a model prayer to adopt and adapt for their own private prayers, Jesus proceeded to teach them about prayer in Luke 11:5-13. The first story He told involved a lesser-to-greater analogy. If an inconvenienced and grumpy neighbor can be counted on to get out of bed and help another in need (see Luke 11:5-8), how much more can God the Father be trusted to answer when we ask, seek, and knock (see verses 9-11). He is never inconvenienced by our asking, and He's never in bed!

To reinforce the point, Jesus turned to another lesser-to-greater analogy. Read Luke 11:11-13.

19. What behaviors characterize the way earthly fathers treat their children in this illustration (see verses 11-12)?

20. In what ways does our heavenly Father's care outshine the examples we experience on earth (see verse 13)?

21. If we are not careful, our negative experiences with our parents, whether they be many or few, can lead us to write our own lesser-to-greater lessons that lead us to misunderstand the nature of God. For example, if our earthly fathers were distant and expected us to handle problems on our own, we can magnify this mistake and imagine God as distant and unconcerned with us. Are there ways in which your relationship to your own parents has interfered with

an accurate view or heartfelt acceptance of God as your Father? If so, what are those ways?

22. How might you counteract the tendency to misapprehend God by projecting your parents' mistakes onto Him?

CALLING GOD NAMES—THE NEXT STEP

Throughout *Calling God Names*, you've learned to think and talk about God by name—by the names He revealed to us. The good news of the Bible is that we don't have to invent lofty and ennobling thoughts about God. We simply have to receive what God has communicated about what is real—the truth.

Now you really know who God is, who He's revealed Himself to be in the Scriptures. It is only left to you to begin calling out to Him in prayer and telling others about His nature.

23. How have your perspective and prayers changed over the course of these weeks as you have focused more attention on God's names?

24. What difficulties have you experienced addressing God directly as the Holy One, the Jealous One, and so on?

25. What name of God do you think your two closest non-believing friends or family members need to hear about?

When could you identify God by that name in conversation with them?

26. Write out every name of God we have studied. Beside each, give one key lesson you have learned about God's nature.

MEMORIZE THIS MESSAGE

You have received the Spirit of adoption as sons, by whom we cry, "Abba! Father!" The Spirit himself bears witness with our spirit that we are children of God. (Romans 8:15-16)

WORSHIP IN THESE WORDS

The following song, "Canticle of God's Glory," proclaims the tri-unity of God the Father, Son, and Holy Spirit. By His life, death, and resurrection, Jesus affirmed what the Old Testament had indicated. God has been eternally Father to the Son, who shares His nature. All who believe in Jesus receive the Holy Spirit and find welcome into the family.

"Canticle of God's Glory"
Author Unknown

Glory to God in the highest,
And peace to His people on earth.

Lord God, heavenly King,
Almighty God and Father,
We worship You,
We give You thanks,
We praise You for Your glory.

Lord Jesus Christ, only Son of the Father,
Lord God, Lamb of God,
You take away the sins of the world:
Have mercy on us;
You are seated at the right hand of the Father:
Receive our prayer.

For You alone are the Holy One,
You alone are the Lord,
You alone are the Most High,
Jesus Christ
With the Holy Spirit
In the glory of God the Father
Amen.[3]

NOTES

CHAPTER 1: THE HOLY ONE

1. Jerry Bridges, *The Pursuit of Holiness* (Colorado Springs: NavPress, 1978), 19.
2. Reginald Heber, "Holy, Holy, Holy!" (words: 1826; music: 1861), http://www.cyberhymnal.org/htm/h/o/holyholy.htm.

CHAPTER 2: THE MOST HIGH

1. Albert Barnes, "Genesis 4:18: Barnes' Notes on the Bible," *Biblos*, accessed July 2, 2012, http://bible.cc/genesis/14-18.htm.
2. Louis F. Hartman and S. David Sperling, "God, names of," *Encyclopaedia Judaica*, vol. 7, Fred Skolnik and Michael Berenbaum, eds. (Detroit: Macmillan, 2007), 672.
3. [Simon Browne], "Hymn 471: The One God," *A Book of Hymns for Public and Private Devotion*, 15th ed. (Boston: Ticknor and Fields, 1866), 367.

CHAPTER 3: THE MIGHTY ONE

1. *Sabaoth* is a transliteration of the Hebrew word meaning "hosts," the Old Testament term for an organized army of men or angels. With the hymn, Luther intended to draw our worship toward Jesus, who is the ruler or champion of all the arrayed powers of men or angels.
2. Martin Luther, trans. Frederic H. Hedge, "A Mighty Fortress Is Our God," (1853), http://nethymnal.org/htm/m/i/mightyfo.htm.

CHAPTER 4: THE ROCK

1. This is the view the medieval rabbi Rashi took in his commentary on Deuteronomy 32:4 (Stone *Chumash*), and it parallels a

discussion of the virtue of "faith" in C. S. Lewis's *Mere Christianity*, book 3, chap. 11.

2. John Rippon, "How Firm a Foundation," *Hymns for the Family of God* (Nashville: Paragon Associates, 1976), hymn #32.

CHAPTER 5: THE JEALOUS ONE

1. N. J. Opperwall, "Jealousy," *The International Standard Bible Encyclopedia,* vol. 2, ed. Geoffrey William Bromiley (Grand Rapids, MI: Eerdmans, 1979–1988), 972.

2. Adam Clarke, commentary to Exodus 32:4 in *Adam Clarke's Commentary and Critical Notes on the Old and New Testaments,* vol. 1 (New York: B. Waugh and T. Mason, 1835), 443.

3. C. S. Lewis, *Mere Christianity* (New York: Collier Books, 1952), 123.

4. The original wording of the third stanza reads "of Rome." John Wesley objected strongly to the Catholic practice of venerating saints and bowing down before their statues. Yet however much a Catholic shrine might resemble pagan idol worship, this author does not believe Catholic doctrine encourages idol worship. I have, accordingly, changed the wording of the third stanza to "of earth," though I do not know that Wesley would do so today.

5. John Wesley, "A Word to a Protestant" in *The Works of the Reverend John Wesley,* vol. 6 (New York: B. Waugh and T. Mason, 1835), 371–372.

CHAPTER 6: THE LORD

1. I am indebted to Nathan Stone for his study of the significance of *Adonai* in *Names of God* (Chicago: Moody Press, 1944), 43–56.

2. S. E. Johnson, "Lord (CHRIST)" in Keith R. Crim and G. A. Buttrick, eds. *The Interpreter's Dictionary of the Bible* (Nashville: Abingdon, 1962), 151.

3. "All Hail the Power of Jesus' Name," Wikipedia, http://en.wikipedia.org/wiki/AllHailthePowerofJesus'Name.

CHAPTER 7: THE FATHER

1. *Hymns for the Family of God* (Nashville: Paragon Associates, Inc., 1976), hymn #138.

2. H. B. Kuhn, "God, Names Of; Names for God in the NT," in Merrill C. Tenney, ed. *The Zondervan Pictorial Encyclopedia of the Bible*, vol. 2 (Grand Rapids, MI: Zondervan, 1975), 764.

3. "Canticle of God's Glory," *The United Methodist Hymnal: Book of United Methodist Worship* (Nashville: The United Methodist Publishing House, 1989), hymn #83.

ABOUT THE AUTHOR

NORMAN HUBBARD graduated from Auburn University with a BA in literature and an MA in linguistics. He currently serves as the campus director for The Navigators at the University of Illinois at Urbana-Champaign. Norman and his wife, Katie, have four school-aged children.

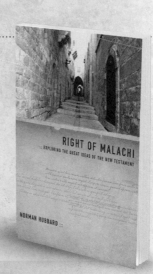

NavPress - A Ministry of The Navigators

Wherever you are in your spiritual journey,
NavPress will help you grow.

*T*he NavPress mission is to advance the calling of The Navigators by publishing life-transforming products that are biblically rooted, culturally relevant, and highly practical.

www.NavPress.com   1-800-366-7788

NAVPRESS⬤
Discipleship Inside Out®